MW00957976

Kanji 100:
Learn the Most Useful Kanji in Japanese

Clay and Yumi Boutwell

Copyright © 2010-2020 Kotoba Books
www.TheJapanShop.com
www.TheJapanesePage.com

ISBN: 148251981X
ISBN-13: 978-1482519815

Makoto Monthly E-Zine for Learners of Japanese

KANJI—an Introduction

There are over 2,000 kanji needed to be literate in Japanese. But in reality, knowing just a couple hundred will allow you to read most anything with the aid of a dictionary. Very few foreigners have mastered kanji. Could you be one of them?

Kanji make up the third part of the Japanese writing system after Hiragana and Katakana. Imported from China, at several stages, hundreds of years ago, these characters are used to represent core meanings such as nouns, adjective stems, and verb stems. The adjective and verb stems are usually followed by hiragana called okurigana.

Each kanji possesses two bits of information:

1. Meaning(s)
2. Pronunciation(s)

Basic meaning: day; sun

Pronunciations (Readings)

Kun Yomi (Japanese native pronunciation(s)): ひ *hi*

On Yomi (imported from China pronunciation(s)): にち *nichi*

MEANINGS AND READINGS

Most kanji have a single core meaning (this could be an abstract notion or something more concrete) and two or more "readings" or pronunciations. The readings are either "*on yomi*" or "*kun yomi*." The "*on*" pronunciation was the original Chinese pronunciation—or at least the sounds Japanese people thought were the Chinese pronunciation. The "*kun*" pronunciation represents the native Japanese pronunciation for that particular concept.

Due to changes in sounds over time, some kanji have an impressive number of pronunciations. It is best to learn these sounds by examples which is why we include multiple example words with each kanji in this book.

HOW DO I STUDY KANJI?

You gotta love 'em!

If you don't decide from the beginning to love kanji, I am sure you will end up hating them. There are many, many characters with various meanings and readings, so without a desire to explore, you will become quickly discouraged.

Meanings

Remembering the meanings of kanji is more immediately helpful. The good news is kanji characters are not randomly generated lines.

It isn't random. **Every kanji is made up of parts**, and many of these parts are reused in other kanji. Note: These are often referred to as radicals, but the word "radical" really refers to the traditional kanji parts used in kanji dictionaries. While this list is a great starting point, you should be free to decide which parts to use as a kanji part.

More good news: Many of these kanji parts have a clear meaning since the part is a kanji itself. If you can create a mnemonic story based on the meanings of these kanji parts, even seemingly complex kanji can be learned quickly.

Pronunciations

For studying the pronunciation of kanji, **learn words and note the kanji in context.**

For example, by learning these two very common words you will know the two most common readings for the kanji 新:

- 新しい *atarashii* - new [Kun Reading]
- 新聞 *shin bun* - newspaper [literally, "new hear"; On Reading]

As you learn vocabulary words, take note of the kanji used. Most often, jukugo (words like 新聞 that are two or more kanji stuck together without the okurigana (trailing hiragana)) are On Readings (the pronunciations from China). So, if you see hiragana after the kanji, it is probably the Kun Reading (native Japanese pronunciations). If you don't see hiragana, it is probably the On Reading (from China).

Our suggestions for studying kanji:

1) Create fun mnemonics that will help *you* remember the character. Make it personal and even absurd. This will help make it stick better. For example, the moon 月 looks like the character for sun 日 but with legs. Think of the **moon** trying to run away from the **sun** since it usually only comes out at night. Try to be consistant with your mnemonics since the same kanji part will most likely show up in future kanji.

2) Keep a writing pad with this book. Copy each individual kanji several times while thinking about the kanji parts. While writing them, try to picture the kanji's reading, meaning, and shape in your head while saying your mnemonic story based on the parts.

3) Finally, read! Use the power of a search engine to look for the newly learned kanji in other contexts. It is an exciting feeling to come across kanji that you have just studied.

KANJI STROKE ORDER

There are good reasons to remember the correct stroke order from the very beginning:

1) By following the set order, kanji will look more like it should and therefore be easier to read.

2) You can remember new kanji better by knowing the order to write them.

3) Kanji dictionaries often list kanji by stroke number.

4) Kanji is an art form in Japan and they will know when you cheat!

If you only have time to remember one thing get this:

**START FROM THE TOP-LEFT OF THE KANJI
AND WORK DOWN TO THE BOTTOM-RIGHT.**

RULE #1 : From top to bottom

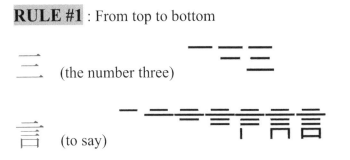

三 (the number three)

言 (to say)

RULE #2 : From left to right

州 (a (U.S. state))　ノ　丿　小　州　州　州

And when you have both a vertical and horizontal **go horizontal first.**

十 (the number ten)　一十

But it wouldn't be fun without exceptions!

田 (rice field)　｜　冂　冂　田　田

王 (king)　一　丁　千　王

RULE #3 : If you have left, right, and center options, work from the center.

水 (water)　亅　刀　水　水

糸 (thread)　㇅　幺　幺　糸　糸　糸

RULE #4 : If there is an outside bit surrounding an inside bit, **the outside comes first.**

国 (country) 丨 冂 冂 国 国

風 (wind) 丿 几 冋 風

Except when the outside is shaped like a "C"

区 (district) 一 フ 又 区

RULE #5 : If there is a vertical line going through other parts, it comes last *or at least later.*

中 (inside, middle) 丨 冂 口 中

書 (write, writing) 𠃌 ヨ 彐 聿 書

And if there is a horizontal line that overlaps other parts, it goes last.

女 (woman) く 女 女

RULE #6 : If there is an "X" or a crossing of diagonals the top-right to bottom-left goes first.

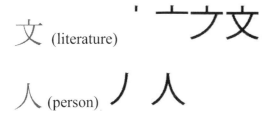

文 (literature)

人 (person)

RULE #7 : If there is a ⻌, it goes last:

進 (proceed)

CONTENTS

Table of Contents

かんじ
漢字

Chapter One: Kanji 1-10

And so begins your kanji journey and it couldn't get any easier!
(...and believe me it won't!)

JLPT N5: 1 / 100 | 1 Stroke

On: イチ
Kun: ひと・つ

Meaning: one; 1

It is a number "1" on its side. Draw the single stroke from left to right.

Examples:

一 *ichi*—one; the number one
一番 *ichi ban*—#1; the best
世界一 *se kai ichi*—the best in the world
一人 *hitori*—one person; alone

どこが一番いいところですか？

doko ga ichiban ii tokoro desu ka?
Where is the best place?

[*ichiban* is often used this way to show the best of something:
ichiban oishii—the most delicious]

Two lines = two, logical!; a little harder, but don't run for the aspirin yet!)
JLPT N5: 2 / 100 | 2 Strokes

On: 二
Kun: ふた・つ

Meaning: two; 2

Two lines make Two!

Stroke Order:

Examples:

二 *ni*—two
第二 *dai ni*—the second
二月 *ni gatsu*—February [the 2nd month]

フロリダの１２月は暑いですか？
furorida no juunigatsu wa atsui desu ka?
Is December in Florida pretty hot?

[Foreign (non-Japan) place names and people's names are written in katakana unless there is a kanji for the name.]

15

Three lines = 3
JLPT N5: 3 / 100 | 3 Strokes

On: サン
Kun: みっ・つ

Meaning: three

Write the three strokes from top to bottom. Remember, the middle is shorter.

Stroke Order:

Examples:

三 *san*—three
三角 *san kaku*—triangle
三月 *san gatsu*—March [the 3rd month]

三月に日本にいきます。
san gatsu ni nihon ni ikimasu.
I'm going to Japan in March.

[The months are easy in Japanese: a number + *gatsu*]

Think of two little legs dangling in a FOUR sided box.
JLPT N5: 4 / 100 | 5 Strokes

On: シ
Kun: よん; よっ・つ

Meaning: four

Stroke Order:

Examples:

四 *yon* or *shi* – four [both pronunciations mean "four" but they are used in different contexts.]
四級 *yon kyuu*—4th grade
四月 *shi gatsu*—April [the 4th month]

四匹のねこを飼っています。
yonhiki no neko wo katteimasu.
I have four cats.

[The verb for owning/having pets is 飼う *kau*—not to be confused with the verb "to buy" which is 買う *kau*.]

This is modern art. 五 is an artist's impression of the number 5. [Well, it kind of looks like the number!]

JLPT N5: 5 / 100 | 4 Strokes

On: ゴ
Kun: いつ・つ

Meaning: five

Stroke Order:

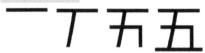

Examples:

五 *go*—five

五月 *go gatsu*—May [the 5th month]

五ヶ月 *go ka getsu*—five months [So far we have seen that adding a number between 1-12 with *gatsu* makes the month names. But here is how to say a duration of months: **# + ka + getsu**—notice it is "*getsu*" not "*gatsu*"]

十五まで数えます。

juugo made kazoemasu.

I can count to fifteen.

[The made here means "until" or "up to (fifteen)"]

A picture of a man stretching his hands and legs is the character for "6."
JLPT N5: 6 / 100 | 4 Strokes

On: ロク
Kun: むっ・つ

Meaning: six

Stroke Order: Make sure the legs do not touch the top.

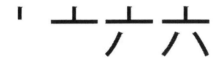

Examples:

六 *roku*—six

六日 *mui ka*—the 6th of the month

六月 *roku gatsu*—June [the 6th month]

六個ほしいです。

rokko hoshii desu.

I want six of them.

[Sometimes *roku* has a sound change before certain sounds. Listen to the sound file to get it down. (see last page for a link to download the sound files)]

A diagonal line through a "L" means "7."
JLPT N5: 7 / 100 | 2 Strokes

On: シチ
Kun: なな・つ

Meaning: seven

Stroke Order: Start with the (almost) horizontal line.

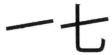

Examples:

七 *shichi* or *nana*—seven
七不思議 *nana fushigi*—the Seven Wonders
七月 *shichi gatsu*—July [the 7th month]

こんばん、「七人の侍」をみます。
konban, shichinin no samurai wo mimasu.
I will watch "Seven Samurai" tonight.

[Seven Samurai is a famous movie by Akira Kurosawa.]

If you have studied katakana, you will notice this looks like *"ha."*
So *HAchi* = 8
N5: 8 / 100 | 2 Strokes

On: ハチ
Kun: やっ・つ

Meaning: eight

Don't confuse this with 人 *hito* (person).
Stroke Order:

Examples:

八 *hachi*—eight
八年間 *hachi nen kan*—8 years
八月 *hachi gatsu*—August [the 8th month]

今月の二十八日は私の誕生日です。
kongetsu no nijuuhachi nichi wa watashi no tanjoubi desu.
The 28th of this month is my birthday.

Don't confuse this one with 力 (power)
JLPT N5: 9 / 100 | 2 Strokes

九

On: キュウ; ク
Kun: ここの・つ

Meaning: nine

Stroke Order: Don't forget to make the hook at the end.

丿 九

Examples:

九 *kyuu* or *ku*—nine
九ヵ月 *kyuu ka getsu*—nine months
九月 *ku gatsu*—September [the 9th month]

今月は九月です。
kongetsu wa kugatsu desu.
This is September.

5 + 5 = 十

JLPT N5: 10 / 100 | 2 Strokes

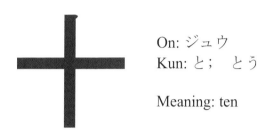

On: ジュウ
Kun: と；　とう

Meaning: ten

Start with the horizontal line.

Stroke Order:

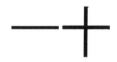

Examples:

十 *juu*—ten
十九 *juu kyuu*—19 [lit. 10 and 9]
九十 *kyuu juu*—90 [lit. 9 and 10]
十二月 *juu ni gatsu*—December [the 12th month]

わたしは十九歳です。

watashi wa juukyuu sai desu.

I am nineteen.

23

Chapter Two: Kanji 11-20

Remember the line over and the number of lines inside the box—that can save some confusion later!

JLPT N5: 11 / 100 | 6 Strokes

On: ヒャク
Kun:

Meaning: hundred

One hundred has a one (━) at top.

Stroke Order:

Examples:

二百 *ni hyaku*—200
三百 *san byaku*—300 [note: sound changes to a harder "b" sound]

ええと、百人くらいいきました。

eeto, hyakunin kurai kimashita.
Let's see... About a hundred people came.

[*eeto* is often heard in spoken Japanese similar to our "umm."]

It looks like a 10 [十] with a slanted line over it. Think of the line as adding two extra 0's: 1000

JLPT N5: 12 / 100 | 3 Strokes

On: セン
Kun: ち

Meaning: thousand

Stroke Order: 1) top (almost) horizontal line; 2) second horizontal line; 3) the vertical line from top to bottom.

Examples:

千円 *sen en*—1000 yen [the 一 *ichi* becomes *"iss"* perhaps because it is easier to say than *"ichisen."* Also yen is pronounced *"en"*]

三千二百 *san zen ni hyaku*—3,200

二千年 *ni sen nen*—the year 2000

これは五千円ほどで買えます。
kore wa gosen en hodo de kaemasu.
This can be bought for about 5,000 yen.

[*hodo* shows the "about" uncertainty.]

The next in numbers. Just add another 0.
JLPT N5: 13 / 100 | 3 Strokes

On: ばん; まん
Kun:

Meaning: ten thousand

Stroke Order: The stroke order for kanji like this is a little different. Start at the top horizontal line. The second stroke is the rightmost one that looks like フ.

Examples:

百万 *hyaku man*—a million (1,000,000) [100 and10,000]
一万円 *ichi man en*—10,000 yen (about $100 USD)
万歳 *ban zai*—hurrah! banzai! hooray! [usually said three times in a row]

はい、一万円ぐらいあります。

hai, ichiman gurai arimasu.
Yes, I have about 10,000 yen.

[This is very roughly $100 USD.]

It looks like a father tying his tie.
JLPT N5: 14 / 100 | 4 Strokes

On: フ
Kun: ちち; とう

Meaning: father

Stroke Order:

Examples:

お父さん *o tou san*—a father
父の日 *chichi no hi*—Father's Day

仕事が終わったら、お父さんはテレビの前で
ごろごろします。

shigoto ga owattara, otousan wa terebi no mae de gorogoro shimasu.

After work, dad just loafs around in front of the TV.

[The honorific "*o*" is usually added to *tousan*.]

Think of a **mother** holding two babies close to her.
JLPT N5: 15 / 100 | 5 Strokes

On: ボ
Kun: はは; かあ

Meaning: mother

Stroke Order:

Examples:

お母さん *okaa san*—a mother; mommy

母の日 *haha no hi*—Mother's Day

保母 *ho bo*—a kindergarten teacher; a nurse

あの子はお母さんにいつもべたべたしています。

ano ko wa okaasan ni itsumo betabeta shiteimasu.

That child is always just clinging to his mother.

[The *betabeta* here gives a sticky effect.]

A picture of a friend giving another friend a hand.
JLPT N5: 16 / 100 | 4 Strokes

On: ユウ
Kun: とも

Meaning: friend

This kanji is often used with words dealing with friendliness.

Stroke Order:

一 ナ 方 友

Examples:

友達 *tomo dachi*—friends; a friend
友情 *yuu jou*—friendship
友好国 *yuu kou koku*—a friendly nation

途中で友達に会いました。
tochuu de tomodachi ni aimashita.
On the way, I ran into a friend.

[*tochuu* is a very useful word meaning "on the way" to any
destination.]

Think of a woman dancing.
JLPT N5: 17 / 100 | 3 Strokes

On: ジョ
Kun: おんな

Meaning: woman; female

A female ninja is called *kunoichi*. If you write hiragana *ku* く, katakana *no* ノ, and the kanji *ichi* 一 you get 女.

Stroke Order:

く　　　夂　　　女

Examples:

彼女 *kanojo*—1) her; 2) girlfriend
女の子 *onna no ko*—a girl
女優 *jo yuu*—an actress

彼は女をナンパばかりする。
kare wa onna wo nanpa bakari suru.
He is always hitting on women.

[*nanpa* means "to hit on" the opposite sex.]

You are making progress!
JLPT N5: 18 / 100 | 7 Strokes

On: ダン
Kun: おとこ

Meaning: man; male

The top part 田 means "rice field" and 力 means "power." So a **powerful man** works in the **rice field**.

Stroke Order:

丨 冂 冂 冃 田 甼 男

Examples:

男女 *dan jo*—men and women
男らしい *otoko rashii*—manly, like a man
雪男 *yuki otoko*—the abominable snowman

赤ちゃんは男の子です。
akachan wa otoko no ko desu.
The baby is a boy.

This is a **person** with no head or arms trying to do a split.
JLPT N5: 19 / 100 | 2 Strokes

On: じん; にん
Kun: ひと

Meaning: person; people

Stroke Order:

Examples:

日本人 *ni hon jin*—a Japanese person [simply add a *"jin"* after many countries]
大人 *otona* – adult; a grown-up [this is an irregular reading]
外国人 *gai koku jin*—foreigner
美人 *bi jin*—a beautiful woman
宇宙人 *u chuu jin*—a space alien

あなたは美人です。
anata wa bijin desu.
You are a beautiful woman.

This is a little child with his arms wide and his mouth open crying for his mommy.

JLPT N5: 20 / 100 | 3 Strokes

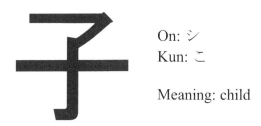

On: シ
Kun: こ

Meaning: child

This is also used with baby animals.

Stroke Order:

フ 了 子

Examples:

子供 *ko domo*—children; child
男の子 *otoko no ko*—a boy [man's child = boy]
お菓子 *okashi*—candy; sweets
子猫 *ko neko*—kitten [child cat]

子供が好きです。
kodomo ga suki desu.
I like children.

Chapter Three: Kanji 21-30
Quite naturally, the sun is a square with a line through it.
JLPT N5: 21 / 100 | 4 Strokes

On: ニチ
Kun: ひ

Meaning: sun; day

The usual word for "sun" is 太陽 *taiyou*.

Stroke Order:

Examples:

ある日 *aru hi*—one day (as in: One day, Little Red Riding Hood...)
毎日 *mai nichi*—everyday
今日 *kyou*—today [irregular pronunciation]
日曜日 *nichi you bi*—Sunday [Notice the two sounds of 日: *nichi* and *bi* (which is *hi* with a sound change)]

毎日、日本語を勉強します。
mainichi, nihongo wo benkyou shimasu.
Everyday I study Japanese.

This is a sun (日) with legs–the moon runs faster around the earth. Therefore it needs legs.
JLPT N5: 22 / 100 | 4 Strokes

On: ガツ; ゲツ
Kun: つき

Meaning: moon; month

Learn these early kanji well. Many of them are found in more complex kanji as radicals.

Stroke Order:

丿 刀 月 月

Examples:

一月 *ichi gatsu*—January [lit. 1st month]
今月 *kon getsu*—this month
月 *tsuki*—the moon
月曜日 *getsu you bi*—Monday

今日は月曜日です。
kyou wa getsuyoubi desu.
Today is Monday.

[All the days of the week end with ~*youbi*.]

Think of it as sparks coming from a person.
JLPT N5: 23 / 100 | 4 Strokes

On: カ
Kun: ひ

Meaning: fire

The left then right sparks are written first.

Stroke Order:

Examples:

花火 *hana bi*—fireworks [note how the *hi* becomes a *bi*]
火花 *hi bana*—sparks [sometimes you can reverse kanji and get a different meaning—note here how the **hana** becomes **bana**]
火山 *ka zan*—volcano [lit. fire mountain]
火曜日 *ka you bi*—Tuesday

あしたは火曜日です。
ashita wa kayoubi desu.
Tomorrow is Tuesday.

Squeeze a river (川) and you get water.
JLPT N5: 24 / 100 | 4 Strokes

On: スイ
Kun: みず

Meaning: water

This kanji as a radical often looks like 氵 and is found with kanji dealing with water.

Stroke Order:

亅　爿　水　水

Examples:

大水 *oo mizu*—flood [lit. big water]
水着 *mizu gi*—swimsuit; bathing suit
水曜日 *sui you bi*—Wednesday

水着を持っていますか？
mizugi wo motteimasu ka?
Do you have your swimming trunks?

This is a tree with two low hanging branches.
JLPT N5: 25 / 100 | 4 Strokes

On: モク; ボク
Kun: き

Meaning: tree

Start with the horizontal line, then vertical. The left and right slanted strokes are last.

Stroke Order:

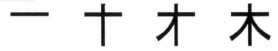

Examples:

木登り *ki nobori*—tree climbing
松の木 *matsu no ki*—pine tree
木曜日 *moku you bi*—Thursday

公園に松ノ木があります。
kouen ni matsu no ki ga arimasu.
There is a pine tree at the park.

Think of gold being buried deep within a hill
JLPT N5: 26 / 100 | 8 Strokes

On: キン; コン
Kun: かね

Meaning: gold; money

Usually *"kin"* deals with gold and *"kane"* means money in general.

Stroke Order:

ノ 人 𠆢 仐 仝 余 余 金

Examples:

お金 *okane*—money
賞金 *shou kin*—prize money
金曜日 *kin you bi*—Friday

お金貸してくれる？
okane kashite kureru?
Will you loan me some money?

It's a **cross** in the **ground**
JLPT N5: 27 / 100 | 3 Strokes

On: ド; ト
Kun: つち

Meaning: earth; ground; soil

Don't confuse this with "gentleman" 士. The **earth is wider than the cross** for this kanji.

Stroke Order:

Examples:

粘土 *nen do*—clay
土地 *to chi*—ground; area; soil
土曜日 *do you bi*—Saturday

土地を売る。
tochi wo uru.
To sell land.

Just as the kanji is made from *ki* (木), so is a book made from trees.

JLPT N5: 28 / 100 | 5 Strokes

On:
Kun: ほん

Meaning: book; counter for long, slender objects

In Japan, you will often see large signs with just this kanji to indicate bookstores.

Stroke Order:

一 十 才 木 本

Examples:

日本 *ni hon*—Japan
絵本 *e hon*—a picture book (for children)
本 *hon*—a book
本屋 *hon ya*—bookstore

本屋はどこですか？
honya wa doko desu ka?
Where is a bookstore?

This is a picture of a person (left) resting against a tree.
JLPT N5: 29 / 100 | 6 Strokes

On: キュウ
Kun: やす・む

Meaning: rest; vacation

As suggested above, the left part (イ) is actually "person" (人)

Stroke Order:

ノ イ 仁 什 休 休

Examples:

夏休み *natsu yasumi*—summer vacation
昼休み *hiru yasumi*—lunch break
お休みなさい *oyasuminasai*—Good night!

休んだほうがいい。
yasunda hou ga ii.
We had better rest.

I know this one looks difficult, but learn it! You'll see it a lot.
JLPT N5: 30 / 100 | 14 Strokes

On: ゴ
Kun: かた・る

Meaning: word; speech; language

It may help to break this down. 言 to speak; 五 the number 5; and the bottom is (口) which means mouth.

Stroke Order:

Examples:

日本語 *ni hon go*—Japanese

物語 *mono gatari*—a story; tale; legend

国語 *koku go*—national language (in Japan, Japanese)

日本語ができます。

nihongo ga dekimasu.

I can speak Japanese.

[Note: the "*dekimasu*" merely shows abiilty, so this could mean "I can speak" or "I understand" or "I can read".]

Chapter Four: Kanji 31-40
This year, study kanji!
JLPT N5: 31 / 100 | 6 Strokes

On: ネン
Kun: とし

Meaning: year

You are making progress. Keep at it.

Stroke Order:

ノ ⺦ ⺦ ⺦ ⺦ 年

Examples:

一年 *ichi nen*—one year
二年前 *ni nen mae*—two years ago
去年 *kyo nen*—last year

今年３０歳になりました。
kotoshi sanjuusai ni narimashita.
I became thirty this year.

[Note: "this year" is "*kotoshi*" not "*kontoshi*".]

Be careful to not confuse this one with 牛 *ushi* (cow).

JLPT N5: 32 / 100 | 4 Strokes

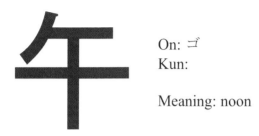

On: ゴ
Kun:

Meaning: noon

This also looks like the previous kanji, year 年.

Stroke Order:

Examples:

午後 *go go*—afternoon (PM)
午前 *go zen*—morning (AM)
午後二時 *go go ni ji*—2 PM

午前のコーヒー

gozen no ko-hi-
Morning coffee

Remember: there is a month in there.

JLPT N5: 33 / 100 | 9 Strokes

On: ゼン
Kun: まえ

Meaning: before; in front of; previous

This versatile word is used with time and space. [before (time) and in front of (space)]

Stroke Order:

Examples:

名前 *na mae*—name
前書き *mae gaki*—preface [lit. before the writing]
二年前 *ni nen mae*—two years ago

お名前は何ですか？
onamae wa nan desu ka?
What is your name?

When you are "behind" (in space) you are "after" (in time) something or someone.

JLPT N5: 34 / 100 | 9 Strokes

On: ゴ; コウ
Kun: うし・ろ; のち

Meaning: behind; after

"*ushiro*" is "behind."

Stroke Order:

丿 ⺈ 彳 彳 徉 徉 徉 後 後

Examples:

最後 *sai go*—the last; the end; conclusion
後ろ *ushiro*—behind
後書き *ato gaki*—postscript; afterword [lit. after the writing]

後ろを見て。
ushiro wo mite.
Look behind (you).

The sun is very important in telling time: 日
JLPT N5: 35 / 100 | 10 Strokes

On: ジ
Kun: とき

Meaning: time

sun 日 + temple 寺

Stroke Order:

丨 冂 冂 日 日⁻ 日⁺ 旷 昨 時 時

Examples:

時間 *ji kan*—time
時々 *toki doki*—sometimes [the 々 character means to repeat]
江戸時代 *e do ji dai*—the Edo Period

何時ですか？
nanji desu ka?
What time is it?

The 門 is the kanji that means "gate." So, in the **interval** of the **gate** there is a **sun**.

JLPT N5: 36 / 100 | 12 Strokes

On: カン; ケン
Kun: あいだ; ま

Meaning: interval; space; room

Similar kanji are 門 gate and 聞 to hear.

Stroke Order:

Ⅰ 冂 冂 冃 冃 門

門 門 門 門 間 間 間

Examples:

時間 *ji kan*—time
昼間 *hiru ma*—daytime
居間 *i ma*—living room

時間がありますか？
jikan ga arimasu ka?
Do you have some time?

Every time you draw this kanji say, "every."
JLPT N5: 37 / 100 | 6 Strokes

On:
Kun: まい

Meaning: every~

Do you see mother? 母 [Page 24.]

Stroke Order:

ノ ヒ 仁 乞 毎 毎

Examples:

毎日 *mai nichi*—everyday

毎朝 *mai asa*—every morning

毎週 *mai shuu*—every week

毎日日本語を勉強します。
mainichi nihongo wo benkyou shimasu.
I study Japanese everyday.

It has two legs so it always walks ahead.
JLPT N5: 38 / 100 | 6 Strokes

On: セン
Kun: さき

Meaning: previous; ahead

This word is used for space and time.

Stroke Order:

ノ　ー　ナ　生　牛　先

Examples:

先生 *sen sei*—teacher
先日 *sen jitsu*—the other day

どうぞ、お先に。
douzo, osaki ni.
Please go first.

It looks like someone with a hat is eating with his mouth wide open **now**.

JLPT N5: 39 / 100 | 4 Strokes

On: コン; キン
Kun: いま

Meaning: now; the present

A very useful kanji.

Stroke Order:

Examples:

今月 *kon getsu*—this month
今晩は *kon ban wa*—good night [lit. as for this night]
今度 *kon do*—next time [you would think this means this time!]

今年３０歳になりました。

kotoshi sanjuusai ni narimashita.
I became thirty this year.

[Note: "this year" is "*kotoshi*" not "*kontoshi*"]

JLPT N5: 40 / 100 | 6 Strokes

On: カ
Kun: なに; なん

Meaning: what

This is a very useful kanji that often shows uncertainty.

Stroke Order:

ノ イ 仁 仁 仃 何 何

Examples:

何人 *nan nin*—How many people?
何か *nani ka*—something
何? *nani?*—What?

何時ですか？
nanji desu ka?
What time is it?

Chapter Five: Kanji 41-50

The shorter bar is **ABOVE** the longer bar
JLPT N5: 41 / 100 | 3 Strokes

On: ジョウ
Kun: うえ; あ・げる; のぼ・る

Meaning: up; to raise up

Don't be shocked at the number of pronunciations (actually there are more!). The best one to remember is *ue*.

Stroke Order:

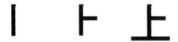

Examples:

机の上 *tsukue no ue*—on (the) desk [lit. desk's above]
上手 *jou zu*—to be good at something [lit upper hand]
年上 *toshi ue*—older; old (in years)

上を見てください。
ue wo mite kudasai.
Please look up.

The shorter bar is **BELOW** the longer bar
JLPT N5: 42 / 100 | 3 Strokes

On: 力; ゲ
Kun: した

Meaning: below; under; down

This one also has several more readings, but *shita* is the most useful for now.

Stroke Order:

Examples:

靴下 *kutsu shita*—socks [lit. shoes under]
地下 *chi ka*—underground; basement
年下 *toshi shita*—junior; younger; young

車の下に猫がいます。
kuruma no shita ni neko ga imasu.
There is a cat under the car.

hidari is left; *migi* is right.
JLPT N5: 43 / 100 | 5 Strokes

On: サ
Kun: ひだり

Meaning: left

Both left (左) and right (右) are very similar. Left has a capital L and right has a mouth.

Stroke Order:

一 ナ ナ 左 左

Examples:

左手 *hidari te*—left hand
左足 *hidari ashi*—left leg
机の左 *tsukue no hidari*—to the left of the desk

左にあります。
hidari ni arimasu.
It is on the left.

hidari is left; migi is right.
JLPT N5: 44 / 100 | 5 Strokes

On: ユウ
Kun: みぎ

Meaning: right

Both left (左) and right (右) are very similar. Left has a capital L and right has a mouth.

Stroke Order:

ノ ナ ナ 右 右

Examples:

右目 *migi me*—right eye
右ページ *migi pe-ji*—right page (of a book)
右手 *migi te*—right hand

右に曲がります。
migi ni magarimasu.
I'm turning to the right.
(in a car, for example)

In order to look at the **sun** from behind a **tree**, you must be facing **east**.
JLPT N5: 45 / 100 | 8 Strokes

On: トウ
Kun: ひがし

Meaning: east

A **sun** [日] character behind a **tree** [木].

Stroke Order:

一 丁 丙 目 自 車 東 東

Examples:

中東 *chuu tou*—the Middle East
東アジア *higashi ajia*—East Asia
東京 *tou kyou*—Tokyo

東京に住んでいます。
toukyou ni sunde imasu.
I live in Tokyo.

"Go west!" said the mouth with legs dangling inside.
JLPT N5: 46 / 100 | 6 Strokes

On: セイ; サイ
Kun: にし

Meaning: west

It would be helpful to learn the directions well as they can be confusing.

Stroke Order:

Examples:

西口 *nishi guchi*—west entrance

関西 *kan sai*—Osaka and surrounding area; Kansai

西ドイツ *nishi doitsu*—West Germany

大西洋 *tai sei you*—the Atlantic

西はどっち？

nishi wa docchi?

Which way is west?

Remember: there is money (￥ *yen*) in the **south.**
JLPT N5: 47 / 100 | 9 Strokes

On: ナン
Kun: みなみ

Meaning: south

Stroke Order:

一 十 ナ 占 肖 肖 南 南 南

Examples:

東南アジア *tou nan ajia*—Southeast Asia
南極 *nan kyoku*—the South Pole; Antarctic
南米 *nan bei*—South America

南に海があります。
minami ni umi ga arimasu.
Down south, there is an ocean.

It looks **like two people sitting** with their back against the **north pole.**
JLPT N5: 48 / 100 | 5 Strokes

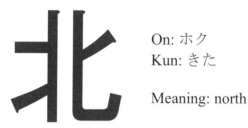

On: ホク
Kun: きた

Meaning: north

Or if it helps... two polar bears sitting back to back.

Stroke Order:

一　丁　丰　北　北

Examples:

北海道 *hokkaidou*—Hokkaido (most northern part of Japan)
北アメリカ *kita amerika*—North America
北京 *pekin*—Beijing (In China)
南北戦争 *nan boku sen sou*—the (US) Civil War

北海道へ行ったことがありますか？
hokkaidou e itta koto ga arimasu ka?
Have you ever been to Hokkaido?

Looks like an **axe** cutting a tree down **outside**.
JLPT N5: 49 / 100 | 5 Strokes

On: ガイ; ゲ
Kun: ほか; そと

Meaning: outside; foreign; other

"Foreigner" is often abbreviated as *gaijin* but this can be considered an insult.

Stroke Order:

ノ　ク　夕　夘　外

Examples:

外国人 *gai koku jin*—foreigner
外国語 *gai koku go*—foreign language

外で遊ぼう。
soto de asobou.
Let's play outside.

JLPT N5: 50 / 100 | 6 Strokes

名

On: メイ; ミョウ
Kun: な

Meaning: fame; famous; name

Stroke Order:

ノ ク タ タ 名 名

Examples:

名前 *na mae*—name
有名 *yuu mei*—famous
平仮名 *hiragana*—Hiragana [the Japanese writing system]

私の名前は〜です。
watashi no namae wa ~ desu.
My name is...

Chapter Six: Kanji 51-60
JLPT N5: 51 / 100 | 10 Strokes

On: コウ
Kun: たか・い

Meaning: high;
tall; costly

Think of this as a picture of a **tall** and **costly** Japanese **building**

Stroke Order:

Examples:

最高 *sai kou*—the highest; the best; supreme [not to be confused with "psycho"]
高校生 *kou kou sei*—a high school student
高いビル *takai biru*—a tall building [note: "*biru*" is taken from the English, "building"]

野菜が高いです。

yasai ga takai desu.
The vegetables are expensive.

JLPT N5: 52 / 100 | 3 Strokes

小

On: しょう
Kun: ちい・さい ; こ ; お

Meaning: small; little

Only three **small** strokes make up this little kanji.

Stroke Order:

亅　小　小

Examples:

小学校 *shou gakkou*—elementary school
小さい家 *chiisai ie*—a small house
小説 *shou setsu*—a novel, a story (fiction)

小さい車がほしい。
chiisai kuruma ga hoshii.
I want a small car.

JLPT N5: 53 / 100 | 4 Strokes

On: チュウ
Kun: なか

Meaning: middle; center; within; inside

It's a line **inside** a box!

Stroke Order:

Examples:

一日中 *ichi nichi juu*—all day long (sound changes from *chuu* to *juu*)

家の中 *ie no naka*—inside the house

勉強中 *ben kyou chuu*—while studying; in the midst of studying

彼は雪の中を歩きました。

kare wa yuki no naka wo arukimashita.

He was walking through the snow.

JLPT N5: 54 / 100 | 3 Strokes

On: ダイ ; タイ
Kun: おお・きい

Meaning: big; large

This is a **big** person (人) with his **great** arms spread wide.

Stroke Order:

一　ナ　大

Examples:

大学 *dai gaku*—university, college
大きい心 *ookii kokoro*—a big heart
大会 *tai kai*—big meet; convention; rally

あなたの頭は大きいです。
anata no atama wa ookii desu.
Your head is big.

JLPT N5: 55 / 100 | 8 Strokes

On: チョウ
Kun: なが・い

Meaning: long; (*chou*—head of an organization; leader)

There are several **long** strokes to make *nagai*.

Stroke Order:

丨 厂 下 丐 戸 長 長 長 長

Examples:

校長先生 *kou chou sensei*—principal (of school)
社長 *sha chou*—a company president
長い道 *nagai michi*—a long road

アマゾン川は世界一長い川です。

amazon gawa wa sekaiichi nagai kawa desu.
The Amazon is the longest river in the world.

JLPT N5: 56 / 100 | 5 Strokes

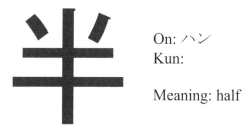

On: ハン
Kun:

Meaning: half

The two top half lines were cut in **half.**

Stroke Order:

Examples:

半ヶ月 *han ka getsu*—half a month
半月 *han tsuki*—a half moon
半島 *han tou*—peninsula [lit. half island]

やっと半分終わった。
yatto hanbun owatta.
Finally, I'm half-way finished.

On: ふん; ぶん
Kun: わ・ける

Meaning: part; portion

The bottom part is a sword (刀) and think of the sword dividing the top **part** into two **parts**.

Stroke Order:

Examples:

半分 *han bun*—half
部分 *bu bun*—a part
気分 *ki bun*—feeling; mood
分かりました *wakarimashita*—I understand

はい、分かります。
hai, wakarimasu.
Yes, I understand.

JLPT N5: 58 / 100 | 8 Strokes

On: ガク
Kun: まな・ぶ

Meaning: learning; study

The bottom is a child (子) and think of the top as his brain waves **learning.**

Stroke Order:

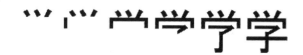

Examples:

科学 *ka gaku*—science
中学校 *chuu gakkou*—middle school; JHS
数学 *suu gaku*—math; arithmetic

数学できません。
suugaku dekimasen.
I can't do math.

JLPT N5: 59 / 100 | 10 Strokes

On: コ ウ
Kun:

Meaning: school

Remember: many **school** buildings are made of trees (木)

Stroke Order:

一 十 オ 木 木

杧 杧 杕 栥 校

Examples:

学校 *gakkou*—school
高校 *kou kou*—senior high school
校内 *kou nai*—within the school; on school grounds

あなたの学校はどこですか？
anata no gakkou wa doko desu ka?
Where is your school?

JLPT N5: 60 / 100 | 5 Strokes

On: セイ; ショウ
Kun: う・む; い・きる

Meaning: birth; life; to give birth; to live

Stroke Order:

丿 ㇌ 牜 牛 生

Examples:

学生 *gaku sei*—a student
一生 *isshou*—all life; a lifetime
人生 *jin sei*—life (human)
先生 *sen sei*—teacher; master; doctor...

先生はあの人です。

sensei wa ano hito desu.
The teacher is that person over there.

Chapter Seven: Kanji 61-70
JLPT N5: 61 / 100 | 3 Strokes

On: サン
Kun: やま

Meaning: mountain

Think of it as a range of three **mountains**, the tallest being in the center.

Stroke Order:

Examples:

火山 *ka zan*—a volcano [lit. fire mountain]
富士山 *fuji san*—Mt. fuji [contrary to popular belief the "*san*" in "*fujisan*" is not "Mr." " *Fujisan*" does not mean, "Mr. Fuji".]
ごみの山 *gomi no yama*—a mountain of garbage
山 *yama*—a mountain

富士山に登ったことがありますか？
fujisan ni nobotta koto ga arimasu ka?
Have you climbed Mt. Fuji before?

JLPT N5: 62 / 100 | 3 Strokes

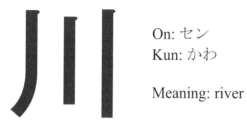

On: セン
Kun: かわ

Meaning: river

This is a picture of water flowing down a stream.

Stroke Order:

Examples:

川 *kawa*—a river
石川県 *ishi kawa ken*—Ishikawa prefecture (on Honshu)
小川 *o gawa*—a stream [lit. small river]

家のうしろに川があります。
ie no ushiro ni kawa ga arimasu.
There is a river behind the house.

JLPT N5: 63 / 100 | 5 Strokes

On: ハク; ビャク
Kun: しろ

Meaning: white

Don't confuse this with 自 which means self—**white has one line** and 自 has two lines.

Stroke Order:

Examples:

白い *shiroi*—the color white

白あり *shiro ari*—termite [lit. white ant]

白鳥 *haku chou*—swan [lit. white bird]

白い猫を飼っています。

shiroi neko wo katte imasu.

I have a white cat.

JLPT N5: 64 / 100 | 4 Strokes

On: テン
Kun: あま; あめ

Meaning: heaven; sky

Heaven is BIGGER than the kanji for big (大). Therefore, there is a line above it.

Stroke Order:

一　二　チ　天

Examples:

天井 *ten jou*—ceiling
天気 *ten ki*—weather
天国 *ten goku*—heaven; paradise
天才 *ten sai*—genius

天気予報はどう？
tenki yohou wa dou?
How's the weather forecast looking?

On: ウ
Kun: あめ; あま

Meaning: rain

Think of the top part as the sky opening to release the rain.

Stroke Order:

Examples:

雨 *ame*—rain
雨水 *ama mizu*—rain water
大雨 *oo ame*—heavy rain

最低！また雨か。
saitei! mata ame ka.
It's the pits... Rain again.

JLPT N5: 66 / 100 | 13 Strokes

On: デン
Kun:

Meaning: electricity; electric powered

Notice the top part is rain, so think of electric lightning.

Stroke Order:

Examples:

電車 *den sha*—(electric) train
電池 *den chi*—a battery
電話 *den wa*—a telephone
電気 *den ki*—electricity; light (from light bulb...)

青木さんに電話してください。
aoki san ni denwa shite kudasai.
Please call Mr. Aoki.

On: キ; ケ
Kun:

Meaning: spirit; mind; power; energy; intention

This is a fun kanji to draw. Sometimes the best way to learn to read a kanji is by drawing it many times.

Stroke Order:

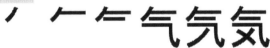

Examples:

空気 *kuu ki*—air; atmosphere
元気 *gen ki*—genki; healthy; full of spirit
電気 *den ki*—electricity; light (from light bulb...)
人気 *nin ki*—popular

あまり元気じゃないです。
amari genki janai desu.
I'm not feeling very well.

JLPT N5: 68 / 100 | 7 Strokes

On: シャ
Kun: くるま

Meaning: car; vehicle

Using your imagination (to the limits of your ability), you may see a **car** with four wheels.

Stroke Order:

Examples:

電車 *den sha*—train
自転車 *ji ten sha*—bicycle
救急車 *kyuu kyuu sha*—ambulance

この車の静かさは驚くべきです。

kono kuruma no shizukasa wa odoroku beki desu.
This car's quietness is amazing.

This is a combination of kuchi (口) [mouth] and tama (玉) [ball]. Sometimes, if the parts that make a kanji are strange, it actually becomes easier to remember! So, get a ball, stick it in your mouth, and think of your country!

JLPT N5: 69 / 100 | 8 Strokes

On: コク
Kun: くに

Meaning: country; nation

You can also think of something being contained by boundaries (countries are lands separated by boundaries).

Stroke Order:

Examples:

韓国 *kan koku*—Korea
外国 *gai koku*—foreign country
中国 *chuu goku*—China

あの国はなぜ貧しいのか？
ano kuni wa naze mazushii no ka?
I wonder why that country is poor?

This is often used instead of the Yen symbol ￥
JLPT N5: 70 / 100 | 4 Strokes

On: エン
Kun: まる・い

Meaning: circle; yen (money)

It seems **money** has **legs** and is always **leaving**.

Stroke Order:

Examples:

千円 *sen en*—1000 yen

円高 *en daka*—a high yen rate

円をかく *en wo kaku*—draw a circle

千円がありますか？

sen en ga arimasu ka?.
Do you have 1000 yen?

Chapter Eight: Kanji 71-80

Most kanji are made of parts. The left side means "a word" and the right side means "tongue."

JLPT N5: 71 / 100 | 13 Strokes

On: ワ
Kun: 話; はな・す

Meaning: a talk; a topic; a story

Kanji about language or words often have the 言 part.

Stroke Order:

Examples:

英会話 *ei kai wa*—English conversation (class)
昔話 *mukashi banashi*—an old tale, legend [note how the "hanashi" becomes "banashi"
手話 *shu wa*—sign language [lit. hand talk]

きのうの話聞いた？

kinou no hanashi kiita?
Did you hear yesterday's speech?

This is a combination of gate (門) and ear (耳). People go to the gate to hear news.

JLPT N5: 72 / 100 | 14 Strokes

On: ブン
Kun: き・く

Meaning: to hear; to listen; ask

Stroke Order:

｜ 「 「 「 「 「 「

門 門 門 門 聞 聞 聞 聞

Examples:

新聞 *shin bun*—newspaper
聞いて下さい *kiite kudasai*—please listen
朝日新聞 *asa hi shin bun*—the Asahi newspaper

きのうの話聞いた？

kinou no hanashi kiita?

Did you hear yesterday's speech?

It looks like a **person reclining** under his **roof eating** something.
JLPT N5: 73 / 100 | 9 Strokes

On: じき；　しょく
Kun: く・う；た・べる

Meaning: food; to eat; relating to food

Think of eating good (良) food.

Stroke Order:

Examples:

食事 *shokuji*—a meal
食べ物 *tabemono*—food; something to eat
食べにくい *tabenikui*—difficult to eat

もう食べた？
mou tabeta?
Did you eat already?

The left part means "a word" and the right part means "to sell."
So a **book** is a **bought word**.
JLPT N5: 74 / 100 | 14 Strokes

On: どく
Kun: よ・む

Meaning: to read

This is another one of those kanji with 言 as part.

Stroke Order:

Examples:

読みやすい *yomi yasui*—easy to read
読書 *doku sho*—reading

読んで下さい。
yonde kudasai.
Please read.

This is one of the very few irregular verbs: *kuru* becomes "*kimasu*" in the -masu form.

JLPT N5: 75 / 100 | 7 Strokes

来

On: ライ
Kun: く・る

Meaning: to come

Stroke Order:

一 丆 丆 平 平 来 来

Examples:

未来 *mi rai*—the future [lit. not yet come]
来月 *rai getsu*—next month
出来る *de ki ru*—able to do something; ready for

あとで来る？
atode kuru?
Will you come later?

Remember this one as the one with a lot of horizontal lines.

JLPT N5: 76 / 100 | 10 Strokes

On: ショ
Kun: か・く

Meaning: book; document; to write

Also remember there is a **sun** at the **bottom**; after all, **you must have light to read!**

Stroke Order:

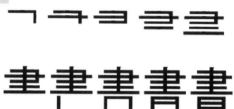

Examples:

図書館 *to sho kan*—library
聖書 *sei sho*—the Bible [lit. holy book]
辞書 *ji sho*—dictionary

図書館はどこですか？
toshokan wa doko desu ka?
Where is the library?

The top part is *me* (eye) and think of the bottom as legs.
Therefore actively using your eyes means to see.
JLPT N5: 77 / 100 | 7 Strokes

On: ケン
Kun: み・る;　み・せる

Meaning: to see; to show

Stroke Order:

丨 冂 冂 月 目 見 見

Examples:

見せて *misete*—show me!
花見 *hana mi*—flower viewing; watching cherry blossoms in April
見える *mieru*—be able to see; visible

あの星見えますか？
ano hoshi miemasu ka?
Can you see that star?

It looks like a side view of a dog (with no tail) ready **to go**.
JLPT N5: 78 / 100 | 6 Strokes

行

On: ギョウ ; コウ
Kun: い・く

Meaning: to go

Stroke Order:

丿 乡 彳 彳 行 行

Examples:

銀行 *gin kou*—bank
旅行 *ryo kou*—a trip; travel

行きましょう。
ikimashou.
Let's go.

This looks like a **mountain on a mountain**—it actually is not—but think of going out to the mountains.
JLPT N5: 79 / 100 | 5 Strokes

On: シュツ
Kun: だ・す ；　で・る

Meaning: to go out; leave

Stroke Order:

Examples:

出口 *de guchi*—exit
出発 *shuppatsu*—to go; departure
思い出す *omoi dasu*—to remember; to recollect

出口はどこですか？
deguchi wa doko desu ka?
Where is the exit?

It looks very much like the kanji for a person (人) but with a little hat on.

JLPT N5: 80 / 100 | 2 Strokes

On: ニュウ
Kun: い・る ； はい・る

Meaning: to enter; to go in; insert

Stroke Order:

Examples:

中入り *naka iri*—intermission (of a play)
入口 *iri guchi*—an entrance
手に入る *te ni iru*—to obtain; to get your hands on...

この入り口はわかりにくいです。
kono iri guchi wa wakari nikui desu.
This entrance isn't easy to find.

Chapter Nine: Kanji 81-90

Think of the kanji as a person sitting at a desk under a roof.
Most **meetings** take place in a **house** with **desks**.
JLPT N5: 81 / 100 | 6 Strokes

On: カイ
Kun: あ・う

Meaning: to meet; meeting

Stroke Order:

Examples:

英会話 *ei kai wa*—English conversation [*kaiwa* by itself means any conversation]
会議 *kai gi*—meeting; conference
教会 *kyou kai*—church

今から会議をはじめる。

ima kara kaigi wo hajimeru.
The meeting will begin now.

Blue moon! You saw me standing alone. I saw you standing at the bottom part of this kanji.

JLPT N5: 82 / 100 | 8 Strokes

On: セイ；ショウ
Kun: あお・い

Meaning: blue

It becomes *aoi* (add the *i*) when placed with a noun —> *aoi ahiru*—a blue duck.

Stroke Order:

Examples:

青空 *ao zora*—blue sky
青森県 *ao mori ken*—Aomori Prefecture
青色 *ao iro*—blue color

私の一番すきな色は青です。
watashi no ichiban suki na iro wa ao desu.
My favorite color is blue.

This kanji has done something **embarrassing** and is **running away** with it's face turned **red.** (see the arms and legs running?)
JLPT N5: 83 / 100 | 7 Strokes

On: セキ； シャク
Kun: あか・い

Meaning: red

Stroke Order:

一 十 土 キ 켜 赤 赤

Examples:

赤ちゃん *aka chan*—a child; infant
赤道 *seki dou*—the equator
赤字 *aka ji*—red ink; in the red; a deficit

私の一番すきな色は赤です。
watashi no ichiban suki na iro wa aka desu..
My favorite color is red.

In the sky the two brightest objects are the sun (日) and the moon (月)

JLPT N5: 84 / 100 | 8 Strokes

On: メイ；　ミョウ
Kun: あか・るい

Meaning: light; bright; to dawn

Stroke Order:

丨　冂　月　日　旫　明　明　明

Examples:

明るい *akarui*—bright; cheerful
発明 *hatsu mei*—invention
説明 *setsu mei*—explanation

今日は明るいです。
kyou wa akarui desu.
Today is bright.

In the fall, many people burn leaves and things with fire (火).

JLPT N5: 85 / 100 | 9 Strokes

On: シュウ
Kun: あき

Meaning: fall; autumn

Stroke Order:

一　二　千　禾　禾

禾　禾′秒　秋

Examples:

秋分の日 *shuu bun no hi*—autumn equinox holiday
秋風 *aki kaze*—autumn breeze

今度の秋、東京に行きます。
kondo no aki, toukyou ni ikimasu.
Next fall, I'm going to Tokyo.

Think of a karate expert jumping in the **air** to break a board in two.

JLPT N5: 86 / 100 | 8 Strokes

On: クウ
Kun: から；そら

Meaning: sky; air; empty

Stroke Order:

丶 丶 宀 宀 空 空 空 空

Examples:

空手 *kara te*—karate [lit. empty hand]
空気 *kuu ki*—air; atmosphere
空港 *kuu kou*—airport
空 *sora*—sky

空を見て。
sora wo mite.
Look at the sky.

Maybe you will recognize *mon* (gate) [門]. I think of a man (in the middle) opening a large gate door by pushing with both arms.

JLPT N5: 87 / 100 | 12 Strokes

On: カイ
Kun: ひら・く；あ・ける

Meaning: open

Be careful to not confuse open with close [閉]. I think of that one as a man kicking the door shut.

Stroke Order:

丨 冂 冂 冃 冃 門
門 門 門 門 門 開 開

Examples:

全開 *zen kai*—full throttle; fully open

ドアを開ける。
doa wo akeru.
Open a door.

It looks like an anvil or some heavy object on top of a heart [心].
When you do something **bad**, your conscience (should) weigh
heavy on your **heart**.

JLPT N5: 88 / 100 | 11 Strokes

On: アク
Kun: わる・い

Meaning: bad; evil

Stroke Order:

一 厂 丆 币 帀 帀

亜 亜 悪 悪 悪

Examples:

悪者 *warui mono*—a bad fellow; someone (something) bad
最悪 *sai aku*—the worst
悪魔 *aku ma* – devil; demon

私が悪かった。
watashi ga warukatta.
I was bad.

The morning is when the moon 月 starts to leave.
JLPT N5: 89 / 100 | 12 Strokes

On: チョウ
Kun: あさ

Meaning: morning

Stroke Order:

一 十 广 古 吉 古

直 車 軒 朝 朝 朝

Examples:

朝日新聞 *asahi shinbun*—Asahi newspaper
今朝 *ke sa*—this morning [irregular pronunciation]
毎朝 *mai asa*—every morning
朝御飯 *asa go han*—breakfast [lit. morning rice]

毎朝新聞を読みます。
mai asa shinbun wo yomimasu.
I read the newspaper every morning.

Think of a young child learning his alphabet under a roof.
JLPT N5: 90 / 100 | 6 Strokes

On: ジ
Kun: あざ

Meaning: letter (from the alphabet); character; mark

Stroke Order:

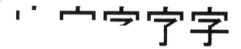

Examples:

文字 *mo ji*—letter
赤十字 *aka juu ji*—Red Cross [*juu ji* is cross]
漢字 *kan ji*—kanji [lit. Chinese character]

この字は何ですか？
kono ji wa nan desu ka?
What is this character?

Chapter Ten: Kanji 91-100

A person doing a split with his legs.
JLPT N5: 91 / 100 | 7 Strokes

On: ソク
Kun: あし ; た・りる

Meaning: leg; foot; to be enough

When you say, "*ashi*" it means both leg and foot. Japanese doesn't distinguish where one starts and the other stops.

Stroke Order:

丨 冂 口 早 早 足 足

Examples:

両足 *ryou ashi*—both legs (both feet)

右足 *migi ashi*—right foot; right leg

満足 *man zoku*—satisfaction

足が棒になった。

ashi ga bou ni natta.

My legs are tired.

[lit. legs have become a stick.]

Of course the kanji that deals with tastes has a *kuchi* (mouth) in it [口].

JLPT N5: 92 / 100 | 8 Strokes

On: ミ
Kun: あじ

Meaning: taste; experience

Stroke Order:

丨 冂 口 口ｰ 口= 吽 味 味

Examples:

味見 *aji mi*—try the taste; have a taste
意味 *i mi*—meaning
趣味 *shu mi*—hobby

ちょっと味見してもいいですか？
chotto ajimi shitemo ii desu ka?
May I have a taste?

JLPT N5: 93 / 100 | 13 Strokes

On: シン
Kun: あたら・しい

Meaning: new; fresh

It may sound strange, but as you progress, you should be able to automatically catch its meaning at a glance. Look at this kanji and think of something new and fresh.

Stroke Order:

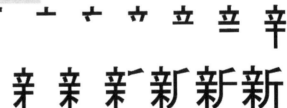

Examples:

新しい車 *atarashii kuruma*—a new car
新聞 *shin bun*—newspaper
新年 *shin nen*—new year

新しい車買いましたか？
atarashii kuruma kaimashita ka?
Did you buy a new car?

This is a **collection** of lines
JLPT N5: 94 / 100 | 12 Strokes

On: シュウ
Kun: あつ・める

Meaning: to collect; gather

Stroke Order:

ノ イ イ´ 仁 仹 仹

隹 隹 隹 隹 集 集

Examples:

編集 *hen shuu*—editing (newspaper, book...)
集める *atsumeru*—to collect, to gather something
集会 *shuu kai*—assembly, group

皿を集めてください。
sara wo atsumete kudasai.
Please collect the dishes.

Think of a loud **older brother** with only a **big mouth** and **two legs**.
JLPT N5: 95 / 100 | 5 Strokes

On: キョウ; ケイ
Kun: あに

Meaning: older brother

Stroke Order:

丨 冂 口 尸 兄

Examples:

お兄さん *o nii san*—big brother (honorific—it changes from "*ani*" to "*onii*")
兄弟 *kyou dai*—brothers

兄はいますか？
ani wa imasu ka?
Do you have an older brother?

JLPT N5: 96 / 100 | 8 Strokes

On: シ
Kun: あね

Meaning: older sister

This kanji is made of two parts: *onna* (woman) [女] and city or market [市] — an **older sister** goes to the **city**.

Stroke Order:

く 女 女˙ 女广 女广 妒 姉

Examples:

お姉さん *o nee san*—big sister (honorific—changes from *"ane"* to *"onee"*)
姉さん *nee san*—girl; older girl
姉妹 *shi mai*—sisters

お姉さんはどこですか？
oneesan wa doko desu ka?
Where is your older sister?

On: ホ; ブ
Kun: ある・く; あゆ・む

Meaning: to walk; to step

The top part is to stop [止] and the bottom means a little [少].
So when you **walk** a long distance you have to **stop** a **little** too.

Stroke Order:

丨　丨丨　丨⊢　止　丿　歩　歩　歩

Examples:

一歩一歩 *ippo ippo*—one step at a time; step by step
散歩 *san po*—a walk; stroll
第一歩 *dai ippo*—the first step

最初の一歩が難しい。
saisho no ippo ga muzukashii.
The first step is difficult.

There **is** a moon.
JLPT N5: 98 / 100 | 6 Strokes

On: ユウ; ウ
Kun: あ・る

Meaning: to exist; to have

Stroke Order:

ノ ナ イ 右 有 有

Examples:

有り難う *arigatou*—arigatou; thank you [almost always written in kana]
公有地 *kou yuu chi*—public land
有名 *yuu mei*—famous

彼は有名になった。
kare wa yuumei ni natta.
He became famous.

JLPT N5: 99 / 100 | 6 Strokes

On: アン
Kun: やす・い

Meaning: 1) safe; peaceful;
2) cheap; inexpensive

Remember this kanji has two different meanings: 1) safe and 2) cheap

Stroke Order:

Examples:

安心 *an shin*—peace of mind
安いもの *yasui mono*—something cheap
安全 *an zen*—safe, safety

これは安いですね。
kore wa yasui desu ne.
Isn't this inexpensive!

The box isn't closed, so the **arrow** 矢 can be removed for
healing.
JLPT N5: 100 / 100 | 7 Strokes

On: イ
Kun:

Meaning: to heal; cure

Stroke Order:

一 丆 匚 三 至 矢 医

Examples:

医者 *i sha*—doctor
医院 *i in*—clinic

はやく！医者を呼んで！
hayaku! isha wo yonde!
Hurry! Call a doctor!

DOWNLOAD THE SOUND FILES

You have finished learning the most important 100 kanji in Japanese. For free resources to help you further your Japanese, please visit http://TheJapanesePage.com. We have many free articles on kanji, grammar, and Japanese vocabulary.

Please check out our store: http://www.TheJapanshop.com for books and other downloads to help you learn Japanese.

To download FREE MP3s for all the example sentences found in this book, please enter the address below in a browser on your computer. The filenames correspond to the numbering found in this ebook.

http://japanesereaders.com/1025

Thank you for purchasing and reading this book! To contact the authors, please email them at **help@thejapanshop.com**. See also the wide selection of materials for learning Japanese at **www.TheJapanShop.com** and the free site for learning Japanese at **www.thejapanesepage.com**.

Made in the USA
Monee, IL
13 October 2023

44511697R00063